Native American Rock Art

Messages from the Past

Native American Rock Art

Messages from the Past

Yvette La Pierre

Illustrated by Lois Sloan

Thomasson-Grant

For Steve, who makes all things possible.

Acknowledgments

With appreciation to Dr. Larry L. Loendorf, for his expertise and guidance; Lawrence E. Beal, Chief of Planning at Petroglyph National Monument, for sharing his site list; the Royal British Columbia Museum in Victoria, Canada, for their definition of culture; and Sharon La Pierre, for providing the inspiration for this book.

Published by Thomasson-Grant, Inc.
Designed by Leonard G. Phillips and Lisa Lytton-Smith
Edited by Rebecca Beall Barns and Susie Shulman

Copyright © 1994 Thomasson-Grant, Inc.
Text © 1994 Yvette La Pierre
Illustrations © 1994 Lois Sloan

PHOTOGRAPHY CREDITS: Cover photograph and pages 8, 9, 18, 21, 26, and 40 © David Muench. Frontispiece and pages 13, 24, 27, 37, 41, and 42 © Tom Till. Pages 15, 33, and 44 © Frank L. Mendonca. Page 31 © Willard Clay.

Illustrations on half-title page, 5, 7, 11, 17, 23, 29, 35, 43, 46, and 48 from Artifact font, Monotype Typography, Inc.

Printed and bound in Hong Kong.

99 98 97 96 95 94   5 4 3 2 1

Library of Congress Cataloging-in-Publication Data
La Pierre, Yvette.
Native American rock art : messages from the past / by Yvette La Pierre ; illustrations by Lois Sloan
p.   cm.
Includes bibliographical references
ISBN 1-56566-064-1
1. Indians of North America–Antiquities–Juvenile literature. 2. Rock paintings–North America–Juvenile literature. 3. Petroglyphs–North America–Juvenile literature. 4. North America–Antiquities–Juvenile literature.[1. Indians of North America–Antiquities. 2. Rock paintings.]
I. Sloan, Lois, ill. II. Title.
E61.L228   1994
709'.01' 130973–dc20   94–13659

Any inquiries should be directed to:
Thomasson-Grant, Inc.
One Morton Drive, Suite 500
Charlottesville, Virginia 22903-6806.
(804) 977-1780.

Frontispiece *Ancient petroglyph of human face with horns and necklace, Leo Petroglyph State Memorial, Ohio.*

THOMASSON-GRANT

TABLE OF CONTENTS

INTRODUCTION

Across North America, from the rocky coast of Nova Scotia to the arid deserts of the Southwest, images of people, animals, and supernatural beings mark stone outcroppings, secret caves, and sharply rising canyon walls. These mysterious works of art were created by early Americans.

Like ancient people in other lands, Native Americans recorded the world around them and their beliefs and myths on stone. For thousands of years, they carved and painted their powerful symbols on rocks, and the pictures they made are known as *rock art*. There are two basic types. *Petroglyphs*, the most common type of rock art, are images pecked or carved on stone surfaces. *Pictographs* are paintings on rocks.

The pictures created by early Americans range in style from simple squiggly lines to elaborate battle scenes with decorated horses and armed warriors. Petroglyphs sometimes depict stick figures, fearsome hunters, or mystical beings. There are pictographs of insects, birds, and animals of all shapes and sizes, even some that are now extinct.

An air of mystery envelops each rock art site, compelling us to wonder about the people who made the images and the messages they may have been trying to communicate. English settlers in Massachusetts Colony were the first Europeans to note prehistoric rock drawings in North America and ponder their meaning. French missionary Father Jacques Marquette, exploring the upper Mississippi River in 1673, saw paintings of horned and winged monsters high on a cliff, which he described in his journal.

The first scientific study of rock art was made in the late 1880s.

Much of what we know about rock art today is the result of studies by scientists called *archaeologists*. Until recently, however, rock art received relatively little attention from archaeologists compared with other *artifacts* left behind by ancient people, such as pottery and weapons. Archaeologists neglected petroglyphs and pictographs for a number of reasons—there was no adequate way to determine their ages, they were too difficult to understand, and there was plenty of work to be done on other archaeological sites.

Now a growing number of scientists across the country devote their studies to rock art, and they are making exciting discoveries. Archaeologists have learned how Native Americans made their pictures by studying the images themselves and the artifacts found near them, such as sticks, bowls, and crude brushes. They even have several methods for determining the approximate age of drawings, ranging from measurements of the plant growth covering them to special laboratory techniques that date the art itself.

The most compelling questions, still to be answered, include why early Americans spent so much time and energy carving and painting on rocks and what the pictures mean. Archaeologists have many theories, but there is still much to learn before we will fully understand these pictures and what they have to tell us about the people who made them so many years ago.

To decipher this story on stone, we must travel back to the beginning, to a time when people first arrived in North America.

ABOVE *Humanlike figures known as anthropomorphs are common images in the Coso Range of eastern California. The pecked lines of their patterned bodies and sunburst heads contrast brightly with the surface of the rock, which is covered with a dark layer of minerals called rock varnish.*

OPPOSITE *A spiral, perhaps a snake, coils inside an image of a bird at the Three Rivers petroglyph site in New Mexico. Rich in rock art, this area has more than 5,000 petroglyphs.*

Chapter 1
The First Americans

Two hunters crouch behind a stone wall, waiting for caribou to come within range. As their prey appears, one of the men suddenly throws his spear, but misses. The other hunter focuses for a moment on an image of a caribou on the rock wall before him, then carefully places his spear along his spear-thrower and steadies the shaft with his thumb and finger. As he hurls his weapon, he feels the great power of this place as it guides his spear to its mark.

Most archaeologists believe that the first Americans walked here across a land bridge that once connected the continents of Asia and North America. Today the two continents are separated by a body of water called the Bering Strait.

One million years ago, when a period called the Ice Age began, it was so cold that water drawn from the oceans into the air returned as snow and sleet. For hundreds of years, the ice piled into huge masses called glaciers. Without the flow of water from the land to the sea, sea levels dropped and the floor of the Bering Strait was exposed, creating a land bridge between the Asian and North American continents.

Across this bridge came caribou, wolves, and foxes. Some 20,000 years ago, and perhaps earlier, humans followed. The first Americans came in search of food, unaware that they had discovered a new world. They soon spread throughout the entire Western Hemisphere, from the Pacific Ocean to the Atlantic, from Alaska to the southernmost tip of South America, settling a new frontier more than 10,000 miles long.

The first Americans discovered a world vastly different from the one we know. Woolly mammoths, mastodons, long-horned bison, camels, tapirs, dire wolves, and giant ground sloths, all now extinct in the Americas, once roamed the continent with countless moose, caribou, buffalo, and other animals. Huge lakes and forests covered the land, and grasses grew thick and waist-high. Large mammals dominated the land until the arrival of the most dangerous hunters of all.

These people were nomadic hunters and gatherers. They lived in small groups, moving often to find new food sources. Women collected plants and trapped small animals to sustain their group, while men hunted larger game. They made excellent weapons, the most powerful of which was the spear-thrower, or atlatl, which allowed a hunter to throw his spear faster, harder, and farther to pierce the tough hide of a mammoth or bison.

As the Ice Age came to a close and the glaciers retreated, the climate became drier. Areas once lush with grass turned to desert, and many of the large mammals that depended on grazing land gradually died out.

As large animals became scarce, the search for food became more uncertain. Eventually, some groups began to raise beans, corn, squash, and other crops. This steady supply of food meant that they

Some 10,000 to 12,000 years ago, early Americans used the atlatl, or spear-thrower, to hunt large animals. The weapon usually had a stop at the back against which the spear rested and leather loops at the front through which the hunter would place his fingers to grip the spear. Small stones tied to the shaft may have been charms for good luck.

were less dependent on hunting and gathering, and they were able to settle into permanent villages. As a result, many early Americans found more time for activities such as making pottery, weaving cloth, and telling stories.

As early Americans spread throughout the continent, they developed into hundreds of different *cultures*. A culture is a complex system including tools, language, arts, and beliefs developed to provide for the material and emotional needs of a group. Based largely on the group's environment—climate, terrain, food sources—cultures vary from place to

place. By the time the first European explorers arrived in the late fifteenth century, Americans in different parts of the country looked different and lived differently from one another and spoke more than a thousand different languages.

While some lived in simple villages, others developed advanced civilizations. In what is now the southwestern region of the United States and present-day Mexico, for example, early people grew much of their own food, built impressive engineering projects such as irrigation canals, created beautiful decorated pottery, and carved and painted skillfully on stone.

Despite their increasingly sophisticated lifestyles, Native Americans did not have an easy life. Growing crops was often as uncertain as hunting, and many threats to their survival—disease, lack of rain, declining herds of animals—were beyond their control. They attributed many of these things to spirits and gods, which often took the form of animals and supernatural beings. Early Americans developed complex ceremonies and rituals to communicate with the gods and ask them for help. Painting and carving on rocks probably played an important part in many of these ceremonies.

These were the people who created rock art throughout North America. Their world was closely tied to the land and the creatures that lived upon it, but it was also a world filled with powerful spirits and symbols.

LEFT Early Americans dedicated a pictograph panel in Canyonlands National Park, Utah, to an activity important to their survival—gathering wild plants and seeds. In this painting, known as the Harvest Scene, the smaller figure appears to be wearing a basket on its back and carrying a tool for gathering wild grain. Rabbits run down the outstretched arm of the figure on the right, and wild plants grow from the middle finger of its oversized hand.

Chapter 2

Images on Stone

With slow, steady movements, the artist dips a frayed stick into a hollowed stone and strokes the rock with paint. In the distance the howl of a wolf pierces the quiet night. But the man continues his work without pause.

At last he finishes his painting and turns from the rock.

A cloud passes, and the full moon casts its light on a life-size figure, dark red, on the rock surface. Wavy lines like serpents decorate the figure's body, and horns protrude from its head. The man glances back over his shoulder to see two staring eyes, round and white, fixed on him. A shiver runs through his body,

and he races down the path to his village.

S imple circles, humpbacked flute players, ghostly rows of square-shouldered creatures, and myriad other images decorate rocks throughout North America. They dance across ceilings of caves, dominate steep cliff walls, and perch on boulders looking out to sea. Many of these curious pictures were made with great skill, while others appear to be mere scrawls. Yet all are enduring records of the first inhabitants of this country.

Rock art images made by carving or pecking on stone are called petroglyphs. Pictures painted on the rock are called pictographs. Sometimes an image combines the two types. A painted figure, for example, may have eyes pecked into the rock.

Most pictographs stand out from the rock in various shades of red, from a bright vermilion to a dull brown-red. Early Americans also painted in black and, less frequently, in white. In a few areas, elaborate, multicolored paintings with greens, blues, and yellows cover cave walls.

Most rock paintings found today decorate caves, rock shelters, and other protected areas. It is possible, though, that a number of images once existed on more exposed rocks and that wind and rain slowly erased them.

Petroglyphs are often found on surfaces that are covered with *rock varnish*, a thin, blue-black layer of clays, minerals, and organic material that forms on rocks after hundreds of years of exposure to weather.

Petroglyphs are the most common type of rock art in North America, occurring by the thousands, especially in the Southwest and the Great Basin area of Nevada and parts of Utah and California. In fact, both pictographs and petroglyphs exist almost anywhere suitable rocks are found in North America. The best places to look for rock art are near the sites of ancient villages, water sources, animal trails, and other places that were frequented by early Americans.

Some locations may have only one or two images, while others have rocks that are so covered with drawings that newer images appear on top of older ones. This is called *superimposition*. Superimposition was fairly common, even when there were unused rock

Some rocks feature only a single image, such as this spiral in Saguaro National Monument in Arizona. Depending on where the image is and who made it, a spiral can represent many different things including water, wind, and journey.

surfaces nearby. This suggests to archaeologists that the choice of certain rocks was very deliberate.

Rock artists chose particular locations for some images. Spirals, for example, could represent water and were sometimes carved or rocks where rain collects. Many archaeologists believe that some rock art locations were sacred areas, or places of power. These might have been places where shamans, or medicine men, communicated with the spirit world.

The images Native Americans carved and painted are as varied as their individual creators. Sometimes early Americans drew abstract shapes. Abstract images are those we can't easily recognize or understand, and include dots, spirals, diamonds, sunbursts, meandering lines, and designs that resemble plants and insects. Though we are not exactly sure what they represent, the designs likely had very specific meanings for the people who made them.

Rock artists also drew recognizable forms such as weapons, people, and animals. More puzzling are the pictures of strange creatures that appear to have come from their visions and legends.

Many drawings of animals are quite realistic, but others feature animals with exaggerated or fanciful features, such as deer with over-size antlers or lizards with antennae.

Some of the most fascinating images in rock art are anthropomorphs, or creatures that resemble human forms. Sometimes rock artists drew them as stick figures and other times as supernatural beings with large, elongated bodies. One might have round, staring eyes and an elaborate headdress, and another only a squiggle for a

According to Native American mythology, a supernatural being called the Thunderbird had the power to make thunder and lightning. Many such creatures, varying widely in style and form, are carved and painted on rocks across the United States.

head. Groups of anthropomorphs loom larger-than-life across canyon walls at some sites in the Southwest.

The Thunderbird, carved and painted on rocks from the Southwest to woodlands in the East, is one of many rock art images from the stories and myths of early Americans. According to legend, this enormous creature caused thunder by flapping its wings, and lightning flashed across the sky when it opened and closed its eyes.

The most widespread design in North American rock art, as well as anywhere else in the world rock art is found, is the human hand—an unmistakable and striking sign for man.

Throughout the thousands of years that Native Americans carved and painted on stone, rock art styles changed as the cultures changed. By the time Europeans arrived, only a few cultures still created rock art. Their pictures, as well as their lives, changed dramatically when the new immigrants settled the country.

Rock artists began to draw more modern images, such as trains, guns, and horses, alongside their traditional designs. Native Americans of the Southwest recorded on stone their own story of Spanish colonization. The first images from this period show Christian churches, crosses, and friars. Later drawings feature battle scenes of Spanish soldiers and Native American warriors on horseback. The square hats worn by the Spanish soldiers contrast with the long, flowing headdresses of the Native Americans.

Few other artifacts have the power to tell such vivid stories and offer such personal glimpses into the lives of early Americans.

OPPOSITE Some rocks are literally covered with designs. The variety of images on Newspaper Rock in southern Utah, from traditional paw prints to modern horses and bridles, illustrates the changing culture of Ute Indians through the centuries. Neighboring Navajo called the outcropping Tse Hane, or "rock that tells a story."

Chapter 3

Making the Rocks Talk

Slowly, carefully, the young man climbs the steep cliff wall, wedging his toes into small cracks and depressions, gripping the surface of the rock with his fingertips. He reaches high for a narrow ledge, but his hand, wet with sweat, slips as he tries to pull himself up.

His trembling body hugs the rock for a moment. Then he wipes his hand on the cloth tied around his waist and tries again. This time he grips the edge of the rock firmly and hoists himself onto the ledge. He studies the smooth, dark rock in front of him and nods in approval. It is the right spot for his carving.

Archaeologists have long believed that the decision of where to carve or paint a design was a very important one and probably depended on the image's intended meaning and purpose. A number of rock art images are so high up on cave ceilings and sheer cliff walls that one wonders why the artist chose such a difficult surface. Some paintings and carvings are on rocks that are easy to see and reach. Still others are hidden away in shelters of stone. An image in a cave probably had a much different purpose than one on a boulder along a well-traveled path.

The decision whether to carve or paint depended largely on the type of rock. Granite, for instance, is generally hard and smooth, making a nice clean surface for a painting. Sandstone and volcanic basalt are softer rocks and are well suited for carving, especially when they are covered with rock varnish.

Rock artists made petroglyphs by chipping away the dark surface of the rock in a particular pattern. This process exposed the lighter colored rock beneath the varnish and gave the design contrast.

The most common way to chip away the rock was to strike it with a hard, sharpened stone. Another common method was to hold a sharpened stone against the rock surface and hit it with another stone, piece of bone, or sturdy hunk of wood. An artist had more control over the design this way. Rock artists also scraped rocks with harder stones to create smooth surfaces and drilled the rock surface by rotating an object against it, making small round holes.

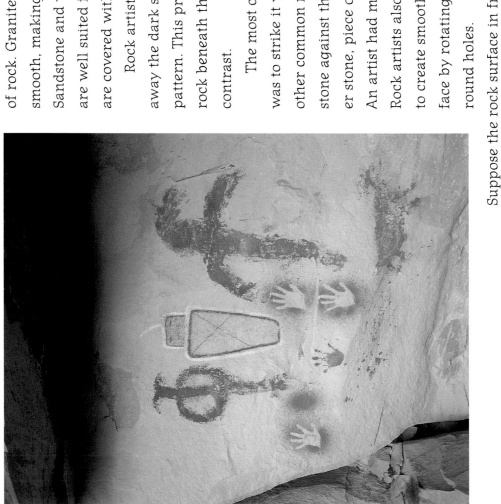

Suppose the rock surface in front of the artist was a light color rather than dark. How would he draw on it? He might scratch into the rock with a sharpened tool made of stone or bone; archaeologists have found stones and other tools at rock art sites that were ground smooth on one side and were the right size for making grooves. The artist might choose to draw directly on the rock with a piece of charcoal.

But more likely, he would choose to paint his design.

To make pictographs, artists had to mix their own paint. Native Americans used minerals and plants they found around them to make paints of different colors. Red, black, and white were the most common paint colors. Red paint was almost universally made from ocher—earth stained red by iron ore. Black paint could be made from charcoal, and white from minerals like gypsum and kaolin or from chalky deposits formed from fossil seashells.

Occasionally, Native Americans found substances to make more vivid colors including yellow, orange, and bright blue. Artists could also combine pigments to create other colors and pastel shades of pink, lavender, and pale green, but this was not a common practice.

After choosing a pigment source, an artist ground the substance into a fine powder and mixed it with a liquid. It is not as easy for scientists to identify the liquid element of the paints, but early Americans probably used animal or plant oils, vegetable juices, milk, blood, and water.

Artists used small stone mortars, bowls, and seashells to grind, mix, and hold the paint. At some sites, the artist's palette was a depression ground into the rock below the painting.

Rock artists could paint the rock by simply dipping a finger or a sharpened stick into the paint. They may have painted larger areas by wrapping a corn husk around a finger or using a brush made from frayed ends of twigs or plants. Some of these brushes and other tools used by rock artists have been found near rock art sites.

The surfaces carved or painted by Native Americans weren't

as smooth and clean as paper or canvas, so artists often planned their drawings to incorporate the natural bumps and colors of the rock's surface. A depression in the rock, for instance, might become a cougar's eye or a spot on a lizard's back.

In some areas, the rocks are covered with handprints that the artists made by smearing their hands with paint and pressing them against the stone. Sometimes they pressed a clean hand on the rock first, then blew pigment around it, which produced a negative image—one in which

the background is colored instead of the image itself.

In some cases, pictographs were repainted at a later date. Perhaps someone intended to make an old, weathered image look new again. At other times, artists wiped away old images to make way for new drawings, or simply painted or carved right on top of them.

It might seem unfortunate that Native Americans "threw away" old pictures like that, but for an archaeologist, the practice provides one of the many clues used to date rock art.

LEFT *When the light is right, carved faces appear along the Connecticut River in Vermont. In contrast to the great number of rock art sites in the western United States—15,000 or more—only a few hundred sites have been found east of the Mississippi River.*

OPPOSITE *Most rock art in North America is fairly simple in style, but the lavish paintings of the Chumash Indians of southern California are an exception. The rare, multi-colored pictographs, which feature strange anthropomorphs, elaborate sun disks, and other complex patterns, are generally hidden away in mountain caves. No longer secret, Painted Cave in the Santa Ynez Mountains, like many other sites, is now marred by graffiti.*

CHAPTER 4
HOW OLD IS IT?

IMAGINE THAT YOU ARE AN ARCHAEOLOGIST, AND YOU HAVE JUST FOUND A PETROGLYPH IN MONTANA. IT IS A RIDER ON HORSEBACK, AND HE CARRIES WHAT APPEARS TO BE A GUN. THE IMAGE IS CARVED ON AN EXPOSED ROCK WALL, SO IT GETS PLENTY OF SUN, RAIN, AND WIND. THE CARVED OUTLINES OF THE RIDER AND HORSE ARE THE SAME COLOR AS THE SANDSTONE ROCK. THE PETROGLYPH IS STILL QUITE VISIBLE, THOUGH BLURRED, AND THE EDGES OF THE DESIGN ARE WEATHERED.

CAN YOU TELL HOW OLD THIS PETROGLYPH IS? NO, NOT EXACTLY. BUT WITHIN THE DESIGN THERE ARE CLUES TO ITS AGE, AND IF YOU KNOW WHAT TO LOOK FOR, YOU CAN COME UP WITH A ROUGH ESTIMATE.

One of the most important clues scientists use to date rock art is the subject the artist depicted. A painting of a figure with a bow and arrow in the eastern woodlands, for example, could not have been made before 1000 BC because that's when early Americans invented that weapon. We know from historians that there were no horses or guns on this continent until the Spaniards brought them in the mid-sixteenth century, so a carving of a man on horseback carrying a gun can't be older than that.

Some methods for determining the age of rock art give only relative ages. This means that a researcher can tell whether one image is older than another, but not a specific age for each. For instance, if a drawing of a figure with an atlatl is next to one of a figure with a gun, an archaeologist can assume that the figure with the gun is the newer drawing because guns were used much later than spears and atlatls.

Similarly, if a drawing of a sheep is on top of, or superimposed upon, a spiral, the sheep is obviously the more recent drawing. An archaeologist might then theorize that all drawings of spirals in the area are older than pictures of sheep. To test this theory, the archaeologist can look for examples of the opposite—spirals superimposed upon sheep. If no such examples exist, the theory is probably correct.

Scientists can roughly estimate the age of a carving or painting based on how worn it is from wind and rain, taking into consideration the location of the drawing. An image on an exposed boulder will wear away more quickly than one in a protected rock shelter.

The amount of rock varnish or *lichen* covering a drawing can help indicate its age, too. Lichen is a plant community of algae and fungus. Like rock varnish, it forms slowly over the surface of some rocks. If an image is almost completely covered by lichen or varnish, that is a good indication that it has been there for a long time. The amount of lichen or varnish covering a drawing can also help scientists determine whether that image is older or newer than other designs near it.

Archaeological artifacts found near rock art also provide clues to its age. Sometimes charcoal, baskets, wooden tools, and other items

Rock artists often created new images on top of older ones, as illustrated by this large bighorn sheep superimposed on older anthropomorphs.

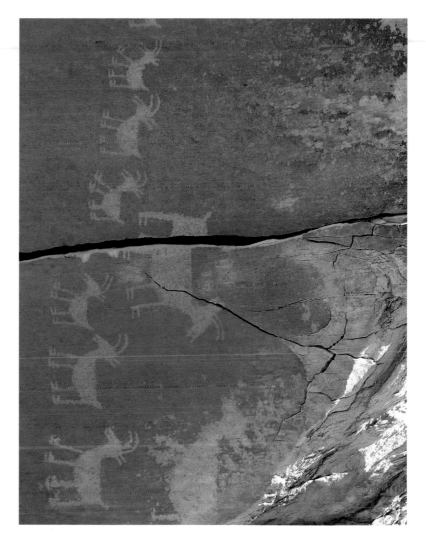

are buried close to the site. A clay bowl found in the ruins of a nearby village might be decorated with images identical to those found on the rocks. Unlike petroglyphs and the weathered rock beneath them, artifacts like these can be dated using a method called carbon-14 dating.

All living organisms contain small amounts of radioactive carbon-14. When an organism dies, the amount of carbon-14 in it decreases at a constant rate. By measuring the amount of carbon-14 left in an object made of once-living material such as bone or wood, scientists can tell its age. Assuming that the images and artifacts found nearby

LEFT *The forces of nature can split stone, here interrupting the march of bighorn sheep across a rock in Petrified Forest National Monument in Arizona. The amount of weathering endured by an image and the rock it is on helps scientists estimate its age. By comparing nearby images—the double-hoofed sheep compared with the faint animal on the right, for example—archaeologists determine which is the more recent image.*

are from the same time period, archaeologists have an approximate age for the rock art.

Since rocks aren't made of living, or organic, substances, carbon-14 dating doesn't work on petroglyphs unless the grooves of the image are covered by a layer of rock varnish. If tiny bits of organic matter, such as pollen grains, are trapped under the rock varnish, scientists can remove a small sample and date it by using a special form of carbon-14 dating called *accelerator mass spectrometry (AMS)*. This technique can also be used to date small samples of paint from pictographs if the paint was made with an organic material, such as charcoal or milk.

AMS estimates age the same way traditional carbon-14 dating does but requires a much tinier sample of material. This is very important because taking samples of an image for dating purposes can damage it forever.

The oldest rock art in North America may have been created 11,000 years ago. Throughout the years, countless images have faded away and others have been erased or covered by later rock artists. Why, then, did early Americans spend so much time and care creating petroglyphs and pictographs that wouldn't last? Perhaps the process of making the picture was more important than the art itself.

CHAPTER 5

DECIPHERING THE STONES

PEERING INSIDE THE CAVE THE BOY SEES ONLY DARKNESS. HE HEARS THE SHARP SOUND
OF ROCK POUNDING ON ROCK AND SOFT CHANTING FROM DEEP WITHIN.
NERVOUSLY FINGERING HIS NECKLACE OF HAWK FEATHERS AND CARVED PIECES OF DEER ANTLER,
HE ENTERS THE CAVE. HE ACCEPTS THE SHARPENED, FIST-SIZE STONE MEDICINE MAN OFFERS
HIM AND CHOOSES A SPOT ON THE CAVE WALL. THERE, BY THE LIGHT OF A SMALL FIRE,
THE BOY BEGINS CHIPPING AWAY AT THE ROCK. AS HE WORKS, HE REPEATS A CHANT,
AND IS SOON UNAWARE OF THE PASSING OF TIME.

HE ISN'T SURE WHETHER HE IS DREAMING OR AWAKE, BUT ON THE ROCK IN FRONT
OF HIM HE SEES A DEER PIERCED BY AN ARROW. HE KNOWS IT IS HIS ARROW,
AND IT IS A GOOD SIGN. HE IS READY FOR HIS FIRST HUNT.

I nterpretation is the process of explaining what rock art images
mean and how they were used by early Americans. This is the most
difficult—and controversial—part of any study of rock art because we may
never know for certain what the drawings mean. While only the artists
themselves hold the keys to unlock the secrets of rock art, archaeologists
do have several tools that allow us to peer through the keyhole.

Perhaps the most important tool for interpreting rock art is an understanding of the cultures that created it. Through the mythologies of the various cultures and the ceremonies still practiced today by Native Americans, we can learn much about what the images mean. For example, archaeologists are better able to interpret petroglyphs of lizardlike creatures found in Arizona because they are familiar with Zuni mythology. According to most versions of the Zuni creation myth, the first people, known as the "moss people," had tails and webbed hands and feet.

Some insight into the meaning and use of rock art has come from Native Americans who themselves took part in ceremonies involving drawing on rocks. Many of those accounts are from the early years of contact between Native Americans and White explorers and settlers, though researchers have learned from Native American rock artists in this century as well.

Objects depicted in rock art, such as food, tools, jewelry, and fig-urines, are sometimes found buried near rock art sites. Archaeologists study these artifacts to learn more about the purpose of the drawings.

Through careful study of rock art and the cultures that created it, most archaeologists agree that many of the rock pictures in North America were made during ceremonies or rituals. Drawing on rocks was one way of asking the gods for all good things, such as rain, good health, fertility, and successful hunts. Wavy lines over tall plants, for example, may have been part of a prayer for rain to help the crops, and the painting of a supernatural being may have been a request for more power or the strength to lead the group, or tribe.

Ceremonies were usually led by a shaman. Still recognized as important members of Native American tribes, shamans use their supernatural powers to communicate with gods and protect and heal other members of the group. They can call upon animal spirit helpers, rise into the sky to meet with gods, and descend to the underworld to fight the demons of sickness and death.

Paintings and carvings of humanlike figures with long bodies and horns or elaborate headdresses are thought to represent shamans or perhaps supernatural beings visible only to shamans. Tiny animals that surround many of these figures may represent spirit helpers. Many Native Americans believe that the images were made by the spirits themselves.

In some cultures, shamans and warriors sought spiritual guidance through solitary vision quests. They fasted to encourage visions that would help them attain special powers and victory in battle. During these rituals, they may have seen many strange figures and animals, which they then painted and carved on rocks. Adolescent boys also sought guidance through vision quests as part of their passage into manhood.

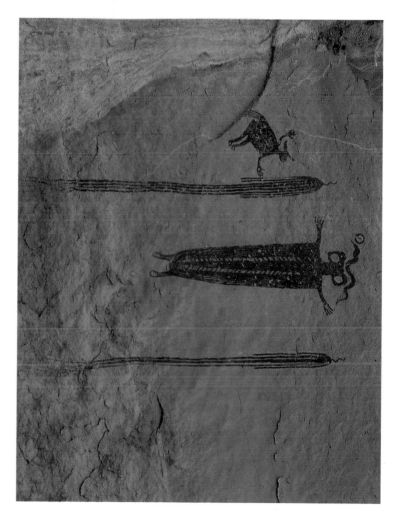

ABOVE *Much of the symbolism associated with shamans, or medicine men, is found in rock art, including supernatural beings with elongated bodies and fancy headdresses. Small animals accompanying them may represent spirit helpers. This carefully painted anthropomorph in southern Utah is flanked by two long, fringed objects and topped by an extremely lifelike snake.*

In many areas, it appears that boys and girls painted on rocks as part of the important ceremonies that prepared them for adulthood. Women, who scientists believe created far less rock art than men, probably carved or painted on rocks as part of rituals to increase their fertility.

Rock art also seems to have played an important part in hunting ceremonies. Native Americans may have carved and painted images of animals and hunting scenes as a way of asking the spirits for help in finding and capturing game. An image of an animal could represent the hunter's prey or the spirit the hunter called upon for help.

Nicks from arrows and bullets cover some drawings of animals in these hunting scenes. Native Americans may have been using the drawings for target practice, or they may have been "attacking" animals during a ceremony to make the real animals more vulnerable before a hunt.

According to Zuni mythology, the first people were lizardlike creatures with webbed hands and feet. They had to live in the underworld until they learned to behave like proper humans.

Early Americans also used rocks like pages in history books to record time, territory, legends, important events, and daily happenings. At many sites, they drew short vertical lines, which could have been tally marks for the number of animals taken in a hunt or the number of days in a vision quest. Some Native American tribes believe that their ancestors drew on rocks as a way of leaving messages for future generations.

Near the Grand Canyon in Arizona, there are entire sandstone boulders covered with images. Hopi Indians once passed by these rocks on their way to the canyon to get salt. Only the bravest Hopi would undertake this journey—the great canyon was also the home of their dead.

Each traveler would stop at the boulders and add another image, called a *clan symbol*, to the rows of designs on the rocks to mark that another member of his group had made the dangerous trip into the canyon. Hopi were still using this site, now known as Willow Springs, when Europeans settled the area. Modern Hopi recognize all but a few of the clan symbols that cover the sandstone boulders.

Native Americans also used clan symbols to mark the boundaries of communal land. A clan is a group within a tribe that is related by blood and is named for the animal or object that is the group's guardian spirit. The clan symbol represents that spirit. The symbol for the Bear clan, for example, is a bear track.

Researchers recognize some rock art panels, particularly in the Southwest and the Great Plains, as Native American versions of events documented by explorers and settlers. One of the finest paintings in Canyon de Chelly in Arizona, for example, features a procession of riders on horseback wearing long cloaks and tall, broad-brimmed hats and carrying long rifles. The painting is believed to be a record of an attack led by Lieutenant Antonio Narbona that took place in Canyon de Chelly in 1805, killing many Navajo.

Recently, researchers have noted that sunlight illuminates spirals and other rock art images only at certain times of the year. It is possible that the images served as solar calendars that marked certain days, such as the longest day of the year or the dates of important ceremonial events.

Hopi Indians pecked more than 2,000 clan symbols, such as corn plants and bear tracks, in rows on sandstone boulders along the way to the Grand Canyon in Arizona.

Not all explanations for rock art are based on archaeological studies. These fantastic images have prompted equally fantastic theories to explain them. Some people claim that aliens from outer space created the rock art of North America. Others, no doubt reminded of Egyptian hieroglyphics, say the drawings are the work of wayward ancient Egyptians, Celts, or Phoenicians.

One of the most common nonscientific explanations is that petroglyphs and pictographs are maps to buried treasures. Though a few abstract images appear to indicate a nearby source of water (a treasure if you are in the middle of the desert and thirsty!), there is no evidence to support this theory.

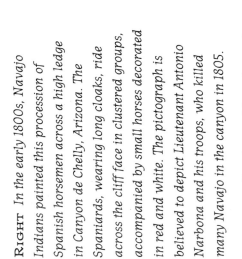

RIGHT *In the early 1800s, Navajo Indians painted this procession of Spanish horsemen across a high ledge in Canyon de Chelly, Arizona. The Spaniards, wearing long cloaks, ride across the cliff face in clustered groups, accompanied by small horses decorated in red and white. The pictograph is believed to depict Lieutenant Antonio Narbona and his troops, who killed many Navajo in the canyon in 1805.*

OPPOSITE *Bee flowers bloom beneath a petroglyph of a square-shouldered warrior holding a shield at Dinosaur National Monument in Utah. Fremont Indians were very skilled artists who typically drew imposing broad-shouldered figures wearing earrings and headpieces.*

Another common myth is that rock art was merely idle doodling by early Americans. Though it is possible that some images were made for recreation, the repetition of designs and styles within certain areas suggests that rock artists had something specific in mind. And it is unlikely that early Americans, who spent much of their time hunting and gathering food, would have made the effort to produce rock art if the pictures had no meaning for them.

So after many years of study, archaeologists have a good idea of what rock art does and does not mean. Still, there remain a great many rock art images for which there are no explanations. Archaeologists are in a race against time to learn more about these images, as petroglyphs and pictographs disappear from rocks throughout North America.

Square-shouldered anthropomorphs and striped animals on a rock wall in southern Utah are slowly losing the battle to the elements. Water seeping within the rock wall weakens the rock, causing whole layers of the stone to break off. The largest figure, on the far right, covers an earlier bug-eyed anthropomorph.

Chapter 6
Vanishing Rock Art

The disappearance of rock art, unlike its meaning and role in the life of early Americans, is not a mystery.

The same natural processes that help researchers determine how old a drawing is can also slowly erase all traces of it. We will never know how many rock drawings were made through the ages because many had already vanished before modern scientists began to record them. And at some point in the distant future, all of these ancient artworks will be gone.

Erosion is the most common natural process that destroys rock art. Unless a rock drawing is in a protected spot, it is exposed to sunlight, rain, frost, and wind, all of which cause the gradual disintegration, or erosion, of the rock surface and the images on it. Billions of grains of sand blown by the wind, for example, work like sandpaper to scour away an image. If erosion can slowly turn a mountain into sand, imagine what it can do to a painting on a rock.

Even rock art in a place protected from weather, such as a cave, is not safe from erosion. Water seeping within rock walls can eventually cause whole layers of the rock to break off, a process called *exfoliation*.

In general, pictographs are more vulnerable to natural forces than are petroglyphs. Plants growing on the rock surface take their toll on rock art, and the organic ingredients in the paints decompose over time.

Though we can't always protect petroglyphs and pictographs from the destructive forces of nature, we can protect them from the destructive acts of humans, such as mining, construction, and *vandalism*, the deliberate harm of public or private property. Unlike the slow work of nature, people can destroy rock drawings quickly and completely.

The building of dams ruins more rock art sites than any other activity; construction destroys some images, and the huge reservoirs of water created when a river is held back submerge the rest.

One of the largest concentrations of rock art in North America once marked cliffs along a stretch of the Columbia River in Oregon and Washington. Thousands of these images are now under water as a result of a series of dams that were constructed along the river. Countless drawings were also submerged in the Glen Canyon of the Colorado River when a dam created Lake Powell.

Other types of construction, including the building of homes and roads, also destroy rock art sites. Even rock art in protected areas is threatened by development. Petroglyph National Monument in New Mexico, established in 1990 to protect the most dense concentration of rock art remaining in the United States, has been bombarded with plans to build a hotel, hiking and horse trails, a nearby airport, and a six-lane highway right through the monument.

Even more disturbing is the destruction of rock art by vandals, who scratch, paint, or spray names, dates, and other graffiti over the ancient designs. In one particularly bad incident, vandals used brushes and a chemical solvent to nearly erase a panel of pictographs at a site in Moab Canyon, Utah. A restoration expert later cleaned the panel, but the paintings will never be the same.

Using crowbars and even dynamite, people remove rock art to

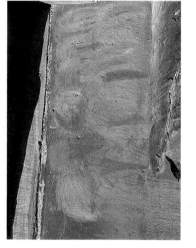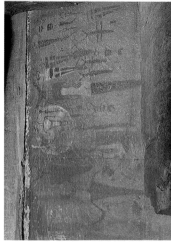

take home as souvenirs or to sell. Often the images, or those around them, are destroyed in the process. Sometimes people damage rock art without meaning to. Climbing on the rocks, taking rubbings of the images, or simply touching the art can harm it.

W hen you visit a rock art site, you can experience the drawings, not by touching them or climbing around them to get a better look, but by letting the rocks talk to you.

First, take a close look at the image. What is it? Is it something you recognize or are familiar with, like a spiral or a bird? What does it mean to you? And how was it made? Check to see if it is very weathered or if the lines are still clean and crisp.

If there's a spot on the rock with no drawings, feel the rock. Is it rough or smooth? What color is it?

Take note of where the drawing is. Is it high on a cliff? Tucked away in a cave? Why do you think the artist chose that particular spot? Now look around the rock art site. Is there a game trail or water source nearby? Can you see any signs of ancient American habitation, perhaps the ruins of dwellings or small pieces of broken pottery? If the drawing was painted, look for stones or mineral deposits the same color that may have been used to make the paint. (Remember to leave everything as you found it.)

Though we cannot be certain of the precise meanings of these ancient designs, we can preserve and respect them, ponder their meanings, and feel some of the power that these places had for early Americans.

Rock Art Sites to Visit

The following is a list of some publicly owned rock art sites in the United States that you can use as a starting point for your own discovery of Native American rock art. For more information on sites in your area, write to:

Petroglyph National Monument
123 Fourth Street, S.W., Room 101
Albuquerque, New Mexico 87102

or the appropriate state office of tourism.

Alabama

Kinlock Knob Petroglyphs, Bankhead
National Forest

Arizona

Canyon de Chelly National
Monument

Homol'ovi Ruins State Park

Painted Rocks State Historical Park

Petrified Forest National Park

California

Barstow Resource Area, Bureau
of Land Management

Chitactac–Adams Heritage County Park,
Santa Clara County

Joshua Tree National Monument

Lava Beds National Monument

Maturango Museum, Ridgecrest
(tours of Little Petroglyph Canyon
by reservation)

Colorado

Dinosaur National Monument

Mesa Verde National Park

Georgia

Track Rock Archaeological Area,
Chattahoochee National Forest

Hawaii

Hawaii Volcanoes National Park

IDAHO
Indian Rocks State Park

KANSAS
Lake Kanapolis State Park

MASSACHUSETTS
Dighton Rock State Park

MINNESOTA
Jeffers Petroglyphs State Historic Site

Pipestone National Monument

MISSOURI
Thousand Hills State Park

Washington State Park

MONTANA
Pictograph Cave State Monument, Department of Fish, Wildlife, and Parks

NEBRASKA
Indian Cave State Park

NEW MEXICO
Chaco Canyon National Monument

El Morro National Monument

Gila Cliff Dwelling National Monument

Petroglyph National Monument

Three Rivers Petroglyphs, Bureau of Land Management

NEW YORK
Allegany State Park

NORTH DAKOTA
Writing Rock Historic Site

OHIO
Leo Petroglyph State Memorial

Mound City Group National Monument

OKLAHOMA
Clem Hamilton State Park

OREGON
Siskiyou National Forest, Daphne Grove

NEVADA
Valley of Fire State Park

TENNESSEE
Montgomery Bell State Park

TEXAS
Amistad National Recreation Area

Hueco Tanks State Historical Park

Seminole Canyon State Park

UTAH
Arches National Park

Canyonlands National Park

Capitol Reef National Park

Fremont Indian State Park

Newspaper Rock State Park

WASHINGTON
Horsethief Lake State Park

Olympic National Park

WISCONSIN
Roche a Cri State Park

WYOMING
Flaming Gorge National Recreation Area

Glossary

Accelerator Mass Spectrometry A special type of carbon-14 dating that requires tiny samples of an object to determine its age.

Anthropomorph A rock art figure with human characteristics.

Archaeologist A scientist who studies historic or prehistoric people and their civilizations through the things the people have built and made.

Artifact An object of historical interest made by humans.

Atlatl (pronounced aht-laht-l) A spear-thrower made of wood or bone with a stop at the end. The extra length of the thrower added speed, force, and distance to the spear.

Carbon-14 dating A method to determine the age of an object by measuring its content of radioactive carbon 14.

Clan symbol A sign that represents the animal or object that is the guardian spirit of a clan. A clan is a group within a tribe that is related by blood.

Culture A complex system of tools, language, arts and beliefs characteristic of a group of people.

Erosion The slow wearing away of the Earth's surface by wind, water, and other natural forces.

Exfoliation The process by which a rock's surface comes off in sheets or layers.

Lichen A plant community of algae and fungus that grows on rocks.

Ocher Earth or clay mixed with iron ore, ranging in color from yellow to red and used as a pigment in paint.

Petroglyph An image made by carving or pecking on rock.

Pictograph An image made by painting on rock.

Rock art Images painted or carved on rock surfaces.

Rock varnish A dark layer of clays, minerals, and organic materials that forms on rocks.

Shaman A person with supernatural powers for healing and communicating with spirits—also called medicine man.

Superimposition One image drawn over another.

Vandalism The deliberate harm of public or private property.

Vision quest A way to communicate with the spirit world through visions brought on by fasting, prayer, and other means.